How to Fight Depression and Win in Life

By Dr Joseph Freeman

2018

Foreword: From Feeling Bad to Feeling Better

When I was young, I suffered lengthy bouts of depression and sadness. My emotional state was partly due to my circumstances and partly the result of an upbringing that taught me to think in negative and disempowering ways.

What helped me escape from depression and overcome it was three things: First, I began to understand why I was depressed. Second, I began to understand my mind and change my ways of thinking. And third, I learned how to set goals and make positive plans for a better future with better circumstances, a future which would make me feel happier.

I discovered that shifting my mind and focus was therapeutic and I have rarely looked back. This book is a work book. I have used examples from my own reading to put this together, but the most important thing is, I have structured this book in three sections, to help you understand your own feelings, then learn to think in an empowered way and finally shift your focus to making a written plan for a good future.

If you do the things this book suggests, I believe you will get some of the same improvement I experienced. So read the book, take the advice, use pen and paper to make notes and set goals and start fighting for a better life and happier feelings. Good luck!

Joe.

Section One:

Recognizing Depression in Yourself.

Depression is a real problem in your life if you suffer at least two weeks of low mood. This low or depressed emotional mood has to be with you wherever you are and whatever you are doing, in most situations you are in, for it to be genuine depression.

You might suffer feelings of low self-esteem, loss of interest in normally enjoyable activities, low energy, and sadness without a reason.

You might suffer from false beliefs or see or hear things that others cannot. You might suffer periods of depression separated by long periods in which you feel normal or you might suffer symptoms which are always present.

Major depression can negatively impact your personal life, your job or your studies, as well as sleeping, eating habits, and general health. If this is your situation, this book is for you.

Keep in mind it is normal to feel sad, lonely, or hopeless at times, such as when you experience a loss or during a time in your life when you are struggling. However, it is a problem when these feelings won't go away, cause physical symptoms, or begin to interfere with your normal daily activities. Untreated depression may continue for months or years, and may even place your life in danger.

This book intends to give you step by step strategies and instructions to fight back against depression and work your way up towards a better emotional state and a happier life.

What Causes Depression?

If you are in a depressed mood, for a sustained period, it is probably caused by a combination of genetic, environmental, and psychological reasons. For example, a family history of the condition, major life changes, the use of certain medications, chronic health problems, etc.

The good news is, most people with depression can be treated with counselling which means changes in your thinking, such as this book aims to help you induce in yourself, can help most depressed people, probably you included.

The cause of major depression is unknown. One theory is that biological, psychological, and social factors all play a role in causing depression. Another idea says that depression results when a pre-existing vulnerability is activated by stressful life events. The pre-existing vulnerability can be either genetic or caused by your views about the world, learned in your childhood.

Childhood experiences such as physical, sexual or psychological abuse are all risk factors for depression. Childhood trauma also relates to the severity of depression, lack of response to treatment and length of illness. However, some people are more susceptible to developing mental illness such as depression after trauma.

Consult a Doctor.

Have you been diagnosed? If not, you need to have a thorough evaluation with a psychiatrist or psychologist before you can be diagnosed with depression. Why? This is because your doctor will carry out a variety of tests, do a physical examination, and have an interview with you to get to the bottom of your symptoms. You should see a doctor and be sure you really have genuine depression, if you have not already done so. However, the ideas and suggestions in this book will be helpful regardless.

Recognizing the Enemy.

To fight your depression, you have to first be sure when you're feeling the symptoms of depression. Depression is different for everyone. You must look for the right signs.

You may have depression if:

- You feel worthless, helpless, or guilty without knowing why.

- You're feeling hopeless about most aspects of your life and can't imagine that anything will improve for you.

- You feel a decrease in your energy levels and are tired no matter what you do.

- You feel restless at night and have trouble sleeping and/or waking up in the morning.

- You've stopped feeling pleasure doing the activities that used to make you happy, such as spending time with friends, pursuing your hobbies, or being intimate.

- There has been a dramatic change in your sleeping habits, such as insomnia, early-morning wakefulness, or excessive sleeping.

- You have lost your appetite or are overeating, but cannot stop.

- It is much easier for you to be alone than to put the effort into interacting with others.

- You constantly feel irritable for no reason.

- You have had thoughts of suicide. If you are thinking suicidal thoughts, seek help immediately. This is absolutely vital. Call a helpline and get help. Your life is everything and you must get help if you have thoughts of suicide.

Learn about the possible causes of depression. Although doctors have not narrowed down one clear-cut reason people experience depression, they tend to see this disorder arise in people with common genetic, biological, psychological, and environmental factors. Your doctor might determine any of the following as being a cause of your depression:

- Addiction to drugs or alcohol. If you have a drug or alcohol addiction, then this may be a cause for your depression. A doctor can help you see if you have an addiction and can tell you the next steps.

- Genetic causes. If depression runs in your family, you are more likely to be depressed. You can discuss whether other people in your family have suffered from depression, even if they were never diagnosed; you can also talk to your parents or other family members to see if people in your family had depression without you knowing.

- A hormonal imbalance. If you have a thyroid problem or other hormonal imbalance, it may be causing your depression.

- Another illness. A doctor can help you see if you're suffering from another illness that can cause or precede your depression, such as an anxiety disorder such as OCD, or even a psychotic disorder such as schizophrenia.

- A side effect of a medication you are taking. If you're taking a medication for another problem, a doctor can tell you if depression is one of the side effects and may be able to switch you to an equally effective medication without this side effect.

- A seasonal disturbance. Some people experience depression as a result of seasonal changes. For example, symptoms might last throughout the winter each year. This form of depression is referred to as seasonal affective disorder (SAD).

Situational Depression.

Before your psychological evaluation, start thinking about some root causes of your depression that may be causing you pain in your everyday life. There's a good chance that specific situations happening in your life, and your reaction to these ordeals, may be contributing to your poor mood. Here are a few things that may be causing or worsening your depression:

- Loss of a friend or loved one. It is normal to grieve after losing someone you care about. However, after a period of time, most people tend to feel better. If your grieving does not seem to lift after months, you may be experiencing depression.

- A failed or unfulfilling romantic relationship. If you are going through a devastating break-up, or are in a relationship that is causing you great pain, then it could be contributing to your depression.

- An unrewarding career. If you feel deeply unhappy, stifled, or even worthless in your current job or throughout your career, then your line of work may be a contributing factor to your depression.

- An undesirable environment. If you live with two screaming, unbearable roommates, or just feel deeply unhappy in your own home or neighbourhood, then your environment may be contributing to your depression.

- Financial reasons. Worrying about making your next rent payment or where your next pay check will come from can be a serious cause of depression if it's a continuing problem.

- "Baby blues." Many women often experience crying spells, anxiety, and mood swings after giving birth. This can be a severe form of baby blues called postpartum depression. Talk to your doctor if your symptoms resemble this condition.

Start a journal. Starting a journal can help you reflect on your depression and feelings and monitor your sensations throughout the day. Make a goal of writing in your journal at least once a day, preferably in the evenings, when you can wrap up whatever the day brought you. Writing in a journal can make you feel more in touch with your thoughts, less alone, and more aware of the things that make you happy or unhappy.

- Writing in a journal will also help you focus and shut off your mind from all the stressful tasks around you.

Improving Your Life

Eliminate toxic or unhealthy relationships from your life. If they are causing you great pain, then it's time to stop making yourself feel worse. If you cannot eliminate a person, such as a family member, spend as little time with that person as possible.

- If there is something in a relationship that is troubling you, have a serious conversation with the person. If you're feeling depressed because you're convinced your husband is cheating on you or that your best friend is stealing your money, then it's time to confront the person and work towards a solution.

Maintain healthy relationships.

Though you may wish to be alone and away from others, it is good for your mood to spend time with others. Rely on your network of friends and family members, as well as your significant other if you have one. Spend as much time as possible hanging out with people who make you feel positive about yourself and the world. Good friends will not only help you cope with your depression by talking about it, but they can make you feel more loved and supported.

- If you have a friend or family member who is suffering from depression, talk to them about it and see what advice they can offer. Just talking to someone who is dealing with the same symptoms can make you feel much less alone.

- If you are in a relationship, make time for romance, or just spending solo time with your significant other. Enjoy yourself and your relationship by scheduling special time to spend with your partner as often as possible.

- Make more time for family. Your family should make you feel loved and supported, so try to spend as much time with them as you can. If your family is across the country, make time for phone calls as much as you can.

Fill your schedule with events and activities you love. Keeping a busy schedule will force you to stay active, focused, and thinking about the next thing on your plate. You can draw up a schedule for each day at the start of the week, or simply plan out each day the night before. Whichever method you choose, make a goal of sticking to it.

Here are some things you should make time for:

- Positive and supportive friendships.

- Exercise.

- Hobbies and interests.

- Time to decompress, write in your journal, or meditate.

- Time to do something silly that makes you laugh.

- Outdoor activities. Don't spend all of your time indoors. Instead, go out into the sun, or do your normal homework or reading in a coffee shop so you feel less isolated.

Find a new passion.

You may not like your current job, but maybe you are not in a position to change your career right now. Finding a new passion can help you feel like you have more of a purpose in life and can give you a reason to wake up in the morning. A passion can be anything you care deeply about, even if it is not something you are good at yet. Here are some great ways to find a new passion: •Explore your artistic side. Sign up for a water-color painting, ceramics, drawing, or pottery class.

- Express yourself through writing. Try writing some poetry, a short story, or even the first chapter of a novel.

- Find a new love for learning a foreign language.

- Discover a new sport. Take a class in karate, ballroom dancing, or yoga.

- Discover a new team sport, such as volleyball or soccer. You will find a new passion while making many friends.

- Discover your love for reading by starting a book club.

Be more generous. Turn your life around after depression by being generous to the people you love and the people in your community. Being generous will help you to increase your self-worth and build greater connections with others around you.

- Do a favor for a close friend. It does not have to be major — if your best friend is having a stressful week, you can offer to pick up her lunch or do her laundry. You will feel better for helping.

- Volunteer at your local library. Help adults and children discover the joy of reading.

- Volunteer at a center for senior citizens, youth, or the homeless, and see what a difference you can make.

- Volunteer in your community by helping clean up your local park. Just spending time in nature can help improve your mood.

Developing Healthier Habits

Improve your sleeping habits. Improving your sleeping habits can be a drastic improvement for your mental health. Work on finding a sleep schedule that works for you. Here are some things that you can do:

•Start going to bed and waking up at the same time every day and night. This will make you feel more well rested and will make it easier for you to fall asleep and wake up.

•Start your day off on the right foot. Spring out of bed and drink a glass of water right away instead of hitting snooze five times before you roll out of bed.

•Develop an effective pre-sleep routine. Wind down in the hour before bed by shutting off your television, putting away your phone or tablet, avoiding loud noises, and reading in bed.

•Limit or eliminate caffeine from your diet, especially after noon. Caffeine will make it harder for you to fall asleep.

•Avoid taking naps that are longer than half an hour, unless you need them — they will only make you feel groggy and more tired.

Exercise.

Exercising for just thirty minutes a day will have a dramatic impact on your physical and mental health. Exercising can give you more energy and make you feel more motivated throughout the day. Find an exercise plan that works for you and stick to it.

•Even taking a walk for just ten minutes a day can help you get some exercise while you reflect.

•Find a gym or workout friend. This will make the experience more enjoyable.

- Set a goal when you work out. Maybe you can have a goal of training for a K, or learning how to do a tricky yoga pose.

Improve your diet. Eating a healthy, balanced diet can also help you beat depression. Even if you're losing your appetite, you need to be determined to eat three meals a day. You don't need to try to lose weight or be incredibly health-conscious when you're dealing with your depression, but eating healthier food regularly will improve your mental and physical state.

- Don't skip meals — especially not breakfast. Eating three meals a day will give you the energy you need to stay positive and focused.

- Add more fruits and vegetables into your diet. Substitute them for sugary snacks or unhealthy junk food.

- Make sure to eat a balance of fruits, vegetables, whole grains, and fish and lean protein every day.

- Let yourself splurge occasionally. You will feel better if you give in to your cravings sometimes.

Think positively.

Being a more positive thinker will help you look at your life and world in a way that fills you with hope instead of despair. To think more positively, you should learn how to recognize your negative thoughts and to fight them with stronger positive thoughts whenever you can. For a jump start on positive thinking, find at least five things to be grateful for and happy about every single day. [] •Try keeping a notebook full of things that you love or make you happy. Every day, write down three or more things, and every week, read about the things you love. This will show you the upside in life and will help you to focus on the positive over negative.

•If you act more positively, you will think more positively. Make a point of talking about the positive things in your life and spending time doing things that make you feel good.

•If you spend more time praising the things that make you smile and less time thinking about the things that upset you or that you don't like, you will think more positive thoughts. Try telling yourself, "Today will be a great day!" or "It's ok, I'm having an awesome day. You can't mess it up!" This can lighten your mood significantly. Always remember to smile, too, because it can make you happier, even if you aren't feeling happy.

Improve your appearance.

Neglecting personal hygiene is a common side effect of depression. While you will not beat your depression by transforming your looks, if you take time to maintain your appearance and hygiene every day, you will feel better about yourself. Shower daily and brush your teeth and hair.

•Work on looking presentable when you face the world, no matter how awful you feel. This will improve your confidence and self-worth.

•If you think that being overweight is a cause of your depression, then setting a goal to improve this aspect of your appearance will improve your mood and outlook.

Considering Your Thoughts and Feelings

Pay attention to your emotions and moods. Depression is a medical condition that prevents the brain from regulating its emotions. Everyone feels down occasionally, but people suffering from depression frequently experience certain emotions, or a combination of them. If you experience these emotions, or if they prevent you from functioning in your everyday life, then it is important to seek help. Some emotions you might feel if you are depressed include:

- Sadness. Are you often sad or low-spirited?

- Emptiness or numbness. Do you feel as though you have no emotions at all, or have trouble feeling anything?

- Hopelessness. Have you felt tempted to "give up", or had trouble imagining any improvement? Have you become more of a pessimist since you began suspecting depression?

- Guilt. Do you often feel guilty for little or no reason? Do these feelings stay with you and interfere with your ability to concentrate or enjoy yourself?

- Worthlessness. Do you have a low sense of self-worth?

- Irritability. Have you been snapping at people or getting into arguments without good reason? A short temper is another example of a mood change sometimes caused by depression, especially among men and teenagers.

- Low energy. Do you often feel tired, unable to perform routine tasks or concentrate, and prone to avoiding active motion?

- Indecisiveness. Do you have difficulty making minor decisions? Does attempting to make decisions make you feel overwhelmed and hopeless?

Section Two:

Taking Charge of Your Mind and Life.

This section of the book offers a simple and easy to understand set of direct step-by-step instructions which you can follow easily to achieve better results in your life.

This section of the book will tackle how to break down time into manageable segments. This section of the book will look at how to clearly decide your purpose in any given segment of time.

Finally this section of the book will give you simple a method of focusing your actions, thoughts and behaviour on your purpose in a segment of time to achieve the best outcome.

This section of the book will also look at long term goals and objectives and some of the useful steps you can take to achieve those long term goals.

Basically, these are the instructions for getting the great life you want.

The Internal Locus of Control

In order to take charge of your life and your time and your results you must first take control of your mind and emotions. If you already have great control of your mind and your emotions, then that is very good but most people could do with more control. If you feel depressed for lengthy periods, you are almost certainly in need of mastering your mind and your thoughts.

The biggest problem for most people is that they are toyed with and played with by outside forces such as their situation or their circumstances as well as the events of each day.

In order to set yourself free from the influence of outside circumstances you must develop what is called the internal locus of control.

An internal locus of control is a control inside yourself.

If you control your mind and your emotions from the inside then outside forces such as situations circumstances and daily events cannot change your emotional state or your mind to drag you down or lift you up.

You are in control of your feelings and thoughts at all times.

This idea of the internal locus of control has often been compared to the difference between a thermostat on the heating unit and the thermometer.

Most people live their life like a thermometer going up or down depending on the environment they find himself in.

But the thermostat is set and it dictates whether the room is hot or cold. Part of the secret of developing an internal locus of control is recognized that almost everything which happens in our life is chosen by us on some level.

We need to except and take responsibility for everything which happens in our life.

Obviously if something happens such as a car accident where another driver is at fault we might find our self thinking we are not to blame for this bad outcome.

However if we look for the area of choice on our own part we will begin to realize that we chose to get behind the wheel and go out on the road driving and although we did not ask to be hit by another car when we went driving we accepted the risk and we accepted that there was a possibility that something bad might happen to us.

Obviously no one wants anything bad happened to them and everyone does all that they can do to avoid anything bad happening but we always except that the risk does exist in every activity and choice in our life.

The internal locus of control is not about blaming other people or other circumstances for what happens to us.

We don't blame other people are feelings either. A person who develops the internal locus of control excepts they own their own feelings and they have the power to choose how they will think feel and react.

The internal locus of control is about not blaming others not apportioning blame or assigning responsibility and control to other people situations or circumstances.

The internal locus of control is about taking charge of your life and your thoughts and your feelings. The internal locus of control is about excepting that you can cause bad things to happen in your life or you can deliberately and intentionally set out to achieve good things in your life.

Obviously no one deliberately causes bad things to happen in their life. Most bad choices made unwittingly in ignorance.

The person who develops the internal locus of control starts to become aware of how their choices shape their life and the risks they take in any circumstance or situation.

They begin to maximize their chances of having good outcomes by behaving with care awareness and responsibility. And they begin to reduce the level of risk by not making silly foolish poor misguided decisions.

The internal locus of control is therefore an essential for practising the ideas in this book about living your life with a folk focus on a clear and meaningful purpose that will lead you to good results.

Goal Setting.

Why is it important to set goals?

In our modern world it seems that there are messages everywhere about following your heart and living according to your passion and striving to make your dreams come true.

Inevitably there are many many comments and messages and books out there on the topic of goals and how to achieve them.

However we must understand this notion of goals and ask yourself the fundamental question of why we should set them and what they can really do for us before we go in any further.

The truth is that there is just too much confusion about the notion of goals and not enough useful and practical guidance on this topic.

The whole reason to have our goal is because of how the human mind works. The single biggest problem with the human mind is that we are easily diverted or distracted of way from what matters.

Even if we have a strong dream in our mind which we want to achieve or make come true we can still be converted away from making that dream become a reality by a number of different things in our life.

When a person takes a pen and paper or on electronic device and writes a goal setting the goal properly it is more than just a note about something we want.

Written and clearly defined goals has a powerful effect on our mind at our behaviour.

If we are able to look at a written goal and use those words as a regular reminder of what really matters it helps the goal to go deep into the back of our mind.

Once a written goal is established and the idea of that goal is firmly embedded at the back of our mind something extraordinary starts to happen.

We begin to look for ways to make that goal a reality in a way that we did not previously. We are even looking subconsciously for ways for that goal to become a physical reality.

And something else happens to. Our mind automatically prioritizes the written goal over all other considerations.

Things which might have previously distracted us away from a completing and accomplishing our goal now begin to fall away as they become second best and our goal becomes out top priority.

A written goal focuses our mind. A goal is not just about getting something either. A goal changes who we are.

Goals have the power to change our behaviour change our personality and bring about real growth in our life in ways that are highly unexpected.

Sit Down and Set A Big Goal

For this activity, take your pen and paper or sit down with your device and write a goal.

Decide what you really want to see in your life in the future and break it down into a goal or at least a set of goals.

Once you have three or four main goal is related to your dream for the future write them down and try to describe them in as much detail.

Try to explain exactly what you want and make the goal as clear as possible.

The bigger and bolder and more amazing and exciting the goal the more power it will have two alter your personality and your behaviour and cause you to grow as a person and lead you toward the amazing day when you can tick off those goals and celebrate the fact that they have come true in your life.

Another thing which will come about in your life as you pursue a goal is the need to have faith. This does not mean religious faith but faith in yourself and in the possibilities which exist for your life and for your future.

This kind of face is important if you want to accomplish your goals and make your dreams come true and become the person you really want to become.

Time and Focus.

It is time to change your focus and start to win in the game of life. In order to win we must understand two very important things. The first thing we need to understand is purpose.

The second thing we need to understand is time. When we try to use time in a way that fits with our purpose we must focus on the right things and in the right way.

If we can do this we will experience success in all areas of life where we use these principles.

This little book will give you a number of step-by-step instructions and clear information about how to master your time management and use your time with clear purpose and approach all tasks with the right focus to win and win big.

This book is not philosophical but a work of practical and applicable instructions which can be used to bring about high levels of achievement in your life.

If you use this book correctly and apply it in your life, you will achieve results which will amaze and astonish other people around you.

So let's begin.

The Time Challenge.

Time and time management are concepts which are widely misunderstood. Everyone has 24 hours in the day and that's all.

How we choose to use those 24 hours is where we have a choice.

If we make wise choices then we will use our time toward a successful happy and fulfilling life. If we make bad choices or even just waste our time then life will become a wasted opportunity.

To understand time we must look at the idea that time can be spent wisely or unwisely.

Spending time unwisely is something everyone is good at. Wasting time only requires ignorance.

To use time wisely toward a good life, a good future, requires planning and purpose and focus.

Defining Your Purpose or Intention

Breaking down time into segments with a single purpose.

Most situations have a set time attached to them. For example if someone begins work at 8 AM and they have a break time at 10 AM in the time. They are dealing with his two hours.

If the job is sales then the purpose is easy to define their purpose is to sell. However there could be more to it. For example if sales involves communicating and connecting with people in a meaningful way by phone or face-to-face and informing people about a product or service during that communication and connection then perhaps it is less important to write my current focus is to sell.

Perhaps it is more helpful to write my current focus is to connect with customers. It's also useful to make some notes to yourself about what this really means.

If you say your purpose is to connect or to communicate then you might moat but connecting means building trust and building understanding through things like small-talk and good humour as well as empathy and understanding for the other person.

However if we are be talking about a time period in which you need to get things done such as getting a target in a very direct and straight forward manner then it could be appropriate to simply write my purpose is to sell.

Winning with Time.

Focus and win! Time and intention, purpose and intention, success principles: this short read will enable you to focus your mind on intention and a purpose at any given time that will maximize your chances of great success in any and all areas of work and life.

Take a pen and paper and write down your current intention using the words "my current intention. "

Write it with as few words as possible, keep it simple and direct.

For example:

My current focus is to read this book.

Now, is that really your focus? Or is your purpose in reading this book to learn?

If so, your intention statement should read:

My current focus is learning.

What we need to understand is the meaning of the old idea of *doing one thing at a time.*

What does it really mean *to do one thing at a time?* What we need to consider is that *a time* really is using the word *time* as an noun and so time is presented in the saying as the indefinite article. Therefore it is one of many. Many times. But do we mean a minute, an hour, a day, a week? Just what do we mean by that?

A time? Do we just mean *right now in the present moment*?

The truth is our time is usually broken up into periods of different lengths and which require a different focus from each other.

So, with this in mind, let's rewrite the saying *do one thing at a time.* Let's change it to *do one thing in time period.*

Or better still, *do one thing in a given time period.* You should do one thing in a clearly defined time period. That is what we must do if we want to really win with time, in our life.

For example: if you are at work, in your job, and you have a meeting to attend, ask yourself a question.

What is my purpose in the meeting?

The time period of the meeting could be one hour. But is it a business update where your boss will bring the team up to speed? Or is it a brain storming session where you will be expected to help solve issues or help come up with ways to accomplish a project or achieve a goal?

If it's a business update, you might write your time and focus statement like this:

Time period of meeting: one hour.

My focus is: listen and note key information.

If it's a brain storming session, you might have a different focus, such as:

My focus is: coming up with helpful suggestions.

Or even just: *My focus is: be helpful.*

A Bad Pen is Better than a Great Memory

One of the most valuable things we can do in order to be very successful in all areas of our life and our work is to understand our purpose and our focus.

In order to really use time effectively we need to understand the idea of prioritizing.

Most time management books suggest that we make a To Do list or a list of tasks and then assign numbers. However there is a more optimal way to use your time.

As we can really only focus on one state of mind and one intention in any given set of hours we should decide exactly what we need to be focused on and doing in that time and the attitude we need to bring to the task.

For example if we are engaged in selling we might decide that our main purpose and focus in each two hour block of time between study work and morning tea and lunch break and afternoon break and the end of the working day is going to be a focus on selling. However there could be blocks of time in our day where we need to focus on other things instead.

If we attend a meeting how focus might be on gathering and noting information.

Our focus could be on paying attention and learning. If we attend a meeting with the intention of brainstorming solutions for strategies for solving a problem or achieving a goal than our focus might be on being helpful and coming up with ideas.

Understanding the need for clearly defined purpose at all times will give us a competitive edge in any area of our life particularly in business.

If we're setting a big goal and striving to achieve it then we also need to break it down into short-term or daily goals.

We need to understand the right focus the right attitude and the right purpose to bring to each block of time each day that we work towards our goal. This is also valuable in other areas of life.

For example, if we are at home with our family we might decide of the time. We are at home and simply spending downtime with family or quality time with family will have a purpose such as be loving be supportive to our wife or partner be supportive to our husband or partner be nurturing and guiding to children and things like that if we are by yourself and we want to relax then perhaps our focus is on winding down and reducing stress and taking care of health and well-being.

If we've had problems in our life how focus might be on such things as managing an illness sustaining or improving health building muscle reducing weight or any other purpose and focus which suits our intention and our goals.

The bottom line is the goals we set for herself should indicate clearly to us what our purpose and focus should be in any given clock of time by setting up a clear awareness of which block of time is in front of us at the present moment and working towards achieving what we need to achieve in that block of time and deciding on a very clear and simply defined purpose we will enjoy a level of success which others do not enjoy.

Always remember to write it down.

For example if we have two hours to spend on a hobby then we might write my current focus is to enjoy my hobby. If we are entering a two-hour time block in which we are going to sell products or services then we might define our purpose for the next two hours as my current focus is to sell.

If we are trying to teach then our purpose might be my current focus is to be nice to students and the helpful and informative to students. If our focus is on providing a service then we might say our focus is to provide good service with a good attitude.

As long as we understand clearly the goal we're working towards in any given block of time the length of the block of time we are in and the kind of purpose we need to focus on in that block of time and the kind of attitude we need to bring to it in order to win we will succeed to a remarkable extent.

Section Three

Working With Your Mind.

Here's what the writer James Allen had to say about the effect of our thoughts upon out circumstances in his classic book *As a Man Thinketh*. Keep in mind, he refers to "a man" but his words apply to all members of Mankind, both male and female. I found James Allen's writing really helped me understand that we can change circumstances instead of just feeling like a victim of them. Please read this passage with care and I believe it will help you too.

Effect of Thought on Circumstances

A man's mind may be likened to a garden, which may be intelligently cultivated or allowed to run wild; but whether cultivated or neglected, it must, and will, bring forth. If no useful seeds are put into it, then an abundance of useless weed seeds will fall therein, and will continue to produce their kind.

Just as a gardener cultivates his plot, keeping it free from weeds, and growing the flowers and fruits which he requires, so may a man tend the garden of his mind, weeding out all the wrong, useless, and impure thoughts, and cultivating toward perfection the flowers and fruits of right, useful, and pure thoughts, By pursuing this process, a man sooner or later discovers that he is the master gardener of his soul, the director of his life. He also reveals, within himself, the laws of thought, and understands with ever-increasing accuracy, how the thought forces and mind elements operate in the shaping of his character, circumstances, and destiny.

Thought and character are one, and as character can only manifest and discover itself through environment and circumstance, the outer conditions of a person's life will always be found to be harmoniously related to his inner state. This does not mean that a man's circumstances at any given time are an indication of his entire character, but that those circumstances are so intimately connected with some vital thought element within himself that, for the time being, they are indispensable to his development.

Every man is where he is by the law of his being. The thoughts which he has built into his character have brought him there, and in the arrangement of his life there is no element of chance, but all is the result of a law which cannot err. This is just as true of those who feel "out of harmony" with their surroundings as of those who are contented with them.

As the progressive and evolving being, man is where he is that he may learn that he may grow; and as he learns the spiritual lesson which any circumstance contains for him, it passes away and gives place to other circumstances.

Man is buffeted by circumstances so long as he believes himself to be the creature of outside conditions. But when he realizes that he may command the hidden soil and seeds of his being out of which circumstances grow, he then becomes the rightful master of himself.

That circumstances grow out of thought every man knows who has for any length of time practiced self-control and self-purification, for he will have noticed that the alteration in his circumstances has been in exact ratio with his altered mental condition. So true is this that when a man earnestly applies himself to remedy the defects in his character, and makes swift and marked progress, he passes rapidly through a succession of vicissitudes.

The soul attracts that which it secretly harbors; that which it loves, and also that which it fears. It reaches the height of its cherished aspirations. It falls to the level of its unchastened desires - and circumstances are the means by which the soul receives its own.

Every thought seed sown or allowed to fall into the mind, and to take root there, produces its own, blossoming sooner or later into act, and bearing its own fruitage of opportunity and circumstance. Good thoughts bear good fruit, bad thoughts bad fruit.

The outer world of circumstance shapes itself to the inner world of thought, and both pleasant and unpleasant external conditions are factors which make for the ultimate good of the individual. As the reaper of his own harvest, man learns both by suffering and bliss.

A man does not come to the almshouse or the jail by the tyranny of fate of circumstance, but by the pathway of groveling thoughts and base desires. Nor does a pure-minded man fall suddenly into crime by stress of any mere external force; the criminal thought had long been secretly fostered in the heart, and the hour of opportunity revealed its gathered power.

Circumstance does not make the man; it reveals him to himself. No such conditions can exist as descending into vice and its attendant sufferings apart from vicious inclinations, or ascending into virtue and its pure happiness without the continued cultivation of virtuous aspirations. And man, therefore, as the Lord and master of thought, is the maker of himself, the shaper and author of environment. Even at birth the soul comes to its own, and through every step of its earthly pilgrimage it attracts those combinations of conditions which reveal itself, which are the reflections of its own purity and impurity, its strength and weakness.

Men do not attract that which they want, but that which they are. Their whims, fancies, and ambitions are thwarted at every step, but their inmost thoughts and desires are fed with their own food, be it foul or clean. The "divinity that shapes our ends" is in ourselves; it is our very self. Man is manacled only by himself. Thought and action are the jailers of Fate - they imprison, being base. They are also the angels of Freedom - they liberate, being noble. Not what he wishes and prays for does a man get, but what he justly earns. His wishes and prayers are only gratified and answered when they harmonize with his thoughts and actions.

In the light of this truth, what, then, is the meaning of "fighting against circumstances"? It means that a man is continually revolting against an effect without, while all the time he is nourishing and preserving its cause in his heart. That cause may take the form of a conscious vice or an unconscious weakness; but whatever it is, it stubbornly retards the efforts of its possessor, and thus calls aloud for remedy.

Men are anxious to improve their circumstances, but are unwilling to improve themselves. They therefore remain bound. The man who does not shrink from self-crucifixion can never fail to accomplish the object upon which his heart is set. This is as true of earthly as of heavenly things. Even the man whose sole object is to acquire wealth must be prepared to make great personal sacrifices before he can accomplish his object; and how much more so he who would realize a strong and well-poised life?

Here is a man who is wretchedly poor. He is extremely anxious that his surroundings and home comforts should be improved. Yet all the time he shirks his work, and considers he is justified in trying to deceive his employer on the ground of the insufficiency of his wages. Such a man does not understand the simplest rudiments of those principles which are the basis of true prosperity. He is not only totally unfitted to rise out of his wretchedness, but is actually attracting to himself a still deeper wretchedness by dwelling in, and acting out, indolent, deceptive, and unmanly thoughts.

Here is a rich man who is the victim of a painful and persistent disease as the result of gluttony. He is willing to give large sums of money to get rid of it, but he will not sacrifice his gluttonous desires. He wants to gratify his taste for rich and unnatural foods and have his health as well. Such a man is totally unfit to have health, because he has not yet learned the first principles of a healthy life.

Here is an employer of labor who adopts crooked measures to avoid paying the regulation wage, and, in the hope of making larger profits, reduces the wages of his work-people. Such a man is altogether unfitted for prosperity. And when he finds himself bankrupt, both as regards reputation and riches, he blames circumstances, not knowing that he is the sole author of his condition.

I have introduced these three cases merely as illustrative of the truth that man is the cause (though nearly always unconsciously) of his circumstances. That, while aiming at the good end, he is continually frustrating its accomplishment by encouraging thoughts and desires which cannot possibly harmonize with that end. Such cases could be multiplied and varied almost indefinitely, but this is not necessary. The reader can, if he so resolves, trace the action of the laws of thought in his own mind and life, and until this is done, mere external facts cannot serve as a ground of reasoning.

Circumstances, however, are so complicated, thought is so deeply rooted, and the conditions of happiness vary so vastly with individuals, that a man's entire soul condition (although it may be known to himself) cannot be judged by another from the external aspect of his life alone.

A man may be honest in certain directions, yet suffer privations. A man may be dishonest in certain directions, yet acquire wealth. But the conclusion usually formed that the one man fails because of his particular honesty, and that the other prospers because of his particular dishonesty, is the result of a superficial judgment, which assumes that the dishonest man is almost totally corrupt, and honest man almost entirely virtuous. In the light of a deeper knowledge and wider experience, such judgment is found to be erroneous. The dishonest man may have some admirable virtues which the other does not possess; and the honest man obnoxious vices which are absent in the other. The honest man reaps the good results of his honest thoughts and acts; he also brings upon himself the sufferings which his vices produce. The dishonest man likewise garners his own suffering and happiness.

It is pleasing to human vanity to believe that one suffers because of one's virtue. But not until a man has extirpated every sickly, bitter, and impure thought from his mind, and washed every sinful stain from his soul, can he be in a position to know and declare that his sufferings are the result of his good, and not of his bad qualities. And on the way to that supreme perfection, he will have found working in his mind and life, the Great Law which is absolutely just, and which cannot give good for evil, evil for good. Possessed of such knowledge, he will then know, looking back upon his past ignorance and blindness, that his life is, and always was, justly ordered, and that all his past experiences, good and bad, were the equitable outworking of his evolving, yet unevolved self.

Good thoughts and actions can never produce bad results. Bad thoughts and actions can never produce good results. This is but saying that nothing can come from corn but corn, nothing from nettles but nettles. Men understand this law in the natural world, and work with it. But few understand it in the mental and moral world (though its operation there is just as simple and undeviating), and they, therefore, do not cooperate with it.

Suffering is always the effect of wrong thought in some direction. It is an indication that the individual is out of harmony with himself, with the Law of his being. The sole and supreme use of suffering is to purify, to burn out all that is useless and impure. Suffering ceases for him who is pure. There could be not object in burning gold after the dross had been removed, and perfectly pure and enlightened being could not suffer.

The circumstances which a man encounters with suffering are the result of his own mental in harmony. The circumstances which a man encounters with blessedness, not material possessions, is the measure of right thought. Wretchedness, not lack of material possessions, is the measure of wrong thought. A man may be cursed and rich; he may be blessed and poor. blessedness and riches are only joined together when the riches are rightly and wisely used. And the poor man only descends into wretchedness when he regards his lot as a burden unjustly imposed.

Indigence and indulgence are the two extremes of wretchedness. They are both equally unnatural and the result of mental disorder. A man is not rightly conditioned until he is a happy, healthy, and prosperous being. And happiness, health, and prosperity are the result of a harmonious adjustment of the inner with the outer, of the man with his surroundings.

A man only begins to be a man when he ceases to whine and revile, and commences to search for the hidden justice which regulates his life. And as he adapts his mind to that regulating factor, he ceases to accuse others as the cause of his condition, and builds himself up in strong and noble thoughts. He ceases to kick against circumstances, but begins to use them as aids to his more rapid progress, and as a means of discovering the hidden powers and possibilities within himself.

Law, not confusion, is the dominating principle in the universe. Justice, not injustice, is the soul and substance of life. And righteousness, not corruption, is the molding and moving force in the spiritual government of the world. This being so, man has but to right himself to find that the universe is right; and during the process of putting himself right, he will find that as he alters his thoughts toward things and other people, things and other people will alter toward him.

The proof of this truth is in every person, and it therefore admits of easy investigation by systematic introspection and self-analysis. Let a man radically alter his thoughts, and he will be astonished at the rapid transformation it will effect in the material conditions of his life.

men imagine that thought can be kept secret, but it cannot. It rapidly crystallizes into habit, and habit solidifies into habits of drunkenness and sensuality, which solidify into circumstances of destitution and disease. Impure thoughts of every kind crystallize into enervating and confusing habits, which solidify into distracting and adverse circumstances. Thoughts of fear, doubt, and indecision crystallize into weak, unmanly, and irresolute habits, which solidify into circumstances of failure, indigence, and slavish dependence.

Lazy thoughts crystallize into habits of uncleanliness and dishonesty, which solidify into circumstances of foulness and beggary. Hateful and condemnatory thoughts crystallize into habits of accusation and violence, which solidify into circumstances of injury and persecution. Selfish thoughts of all kinds crystallize into habits of self-seeking, which solidify into circumstances more of less distressing.

On the other hand, beautiful thoughts of all crystallize into habits of grace and kindliness, which solidify into genial and sunny circumstances. Pure thoughts crystallize into habits of temperance and self-control, which solidify into circumstances of repose and peace. Thoughts of courage, self-reliance, and decision crystallize into manly habits, which solidify into circumstances of success, plenty, and freedom.

Energetic thoughts crystallize into habits of cleanliness and industry, which solidify into circumstances of pleasantness. Gentle and forgiving thoughts crystallize into habits of gentleness, which solidify into protective and preservative circumstances. Loving and unselfish thoughts crystallize into habits of self-forgetfulness for others, which solidify into circumstances of sure and abiding prosperity and true riches.

Focus Your Mind on the Life You Want to Enjoy

As James Allen explains, there is a choice to make and that choice is in our thinking. We need to take charge of our minds and get focused on creating circumstances we like, which will feed back positive feelings to us, rather than being the passive victim of circumstances, if we want to be free of long term depressed feelings.

Now let's take a look at some more tips for setting goals and making them happen.

Everyone has dreams. Whether they are big or small, they have vast importance in our lives. Achieving these goals is related to our happiness and well-being. It is a way to increase self-esteem. The process of striving for our goals can also help us develop into better people. So, whether your dream is to earn a million dollars, become an artist, or be a world-class athlete, don't wait. Start working toward your goal today.

Decide what you want. Your first step is to determine what it is you want to achieve. This can be a big change or small one, but taking some time to think about what you hope to achieve is an important first step to success.

For example, is your goal to be a happier person? To learn to play an instrument? To get good at a sport? To be healthier? All of these are valid goals. It's up to you to decide what you want.

Define your terms. Once you have a general sense of what you want, you need to start thinking about what these goals mean to you. One person's definition of a goal can be very different from another's.

For example, if your goal is to be happier, you need to think about what happiness means to you. What does a happy life look like? What types of things will make you happy?

This applies to less overreaching goals as well. If your goal is to learn to play guitar, what does that mean exactly to you? Will you be satisfied with knowing a few chords so people can sing along with you at parties? Or are you striving to be a classical concert guitarist? These are very different definitions of knowing how to play the guitar.

Ask why. It's important to take a little time to think about why you are setting the goals you've chosen. If you think about your motivations, you may find that you end up wanting to revise your goals.

For example, imagine your goal is to learn to play the guitar. You stop and think about why, and you realize that it's because you think people who play the guitar are popular at school. This doesn't really suggest dedication to the guitar. It might be a good reason to stop and ask yourself if there's another, easier way to get what you really want, which is more social than musical.

Determine if it's possible. Last but not least, you need to decide if your goal is realistic. Sad as it may seem, not every dream can come true. If your goal seems beyond the realm of possibility, it might be time to make a different goal.

Imagine you decide it is your dream to be the worlds greatest basketball player. That's a challenging goal for anyone to achieve, but it might be possible for some people. But, if you're only 5 feet (1.5 m) tall, this goal is probably beyond your reach. This sets you up for failure and discouragement.[5] You can still have fun playing basketball with your friends. But, if you're looking to be the best at a sport, you should probably focus on one where height isn't so important.

Making a Plan

Brainstorm in writing. Once you've set a general goal, you need to start getting more specific and making a plan to reach it. A great first step is to do some free-writing. Get some paper and write down some thoughts about the following topics:

Your ideal future

Qualities you admire in others

Things that could be done better

Things you want to learn more about

Habits you want to improve.

This step is meant to help you fantasize and imagine many possibilities. After a few of these possibilities are out on paper, you can determine which ones are most important to you.

Get specific. Once you've thought about some goals and brainstormed a bit, its time to start getting more specific. Use your notes from the brainstorming session and your definitions from the previous section. Write down some specific things you would like to achieve or do.

A vague goal like, "I want to play better, so I will do my best," is not as effective as a goal like "I want to be able to play my favorite song in six months." Poorly defined end goals or vague "do-your-best" goals are not as effective as specific goals.

Move beyond general goals like "I want to become rich" and focus on specific achievements that will get results. Instead of "I want to become rich," your goal could be "I want to master investing in the stock market." Instead of "I want to play the guitar," your goal could be something like "I want to play lead guitar in a rock band."

It's a good idea to do some more writing here, trying to describe your goals in as much detail as possible.

Consider using the SMART method. One way to specify and evaluate your goals is to use the SMART method. This is an approach to goal setting in which you refine your goals by assessing whether they are:

Specific

Measurable

Achievable

Relevant and

Time-bounded

Rank your goals. Many people have several goals. In fact, in your free-writing, you may have discovered that you yourself are already hoping to achieve more than one goal. If this is the case, it's a good idea to try to rank them in order of importance.

Ranking your goals will help you focus on those that are the most meaningful to you.

For example, you might want to earn a PhD in astrophysics, learn to play classical guitar, read the complete works of Tolstoy, and run a marathon. Trying to do all of these things at once is probably not realistic. Deciding which goals are most important can help you plan for the long and short term.

Part of this process is assessing your level of commitment to each goal. A difficult or long-term goal that you aren't highly committed to is one you are unlikely to achieve.If you only sort of want a PhD in astrophysics, you probably shouldn't make that a priority in life.

Envision the impacts. Spend some time thinking about how each of these goals will affect your life. This will help you determine the benefits of striving for each of your goals.

Thinking in these terms will also help you visualize the process of striving for these goals. This can help boost your motivation.

Create sub-goals. Most goals are more achievable if broken down into smaller tasks. These smaller tasks are sub-goals--little goals that add up to the main goal you hope to achieve.

For example, if you want to learn to play guitar, your first sub-goal might be to get a guitar. Your next might be to sign up for lessons. Next, you will want to learn the most basic chords and scales, and so on.

Creating a schedule for these sub-goals can help you stay focused and keep you on track.In the example above, you might aim to have enough money to buy a guitar in three months. You might plan sign up for lessons a week after that, learn the basic chords in another two months, and so forth.

Identify obstacles. Last but not least, think about what obstacles could stand in the way of achieving your goals. Thinking about this in advance gives you a chance to come up with some ideas about how you will overcome those obstacles.

For example, you might find that guitar lessons are more costly than you can afford right now. This could lead you to think about ways to get more money for lessons. Or, you might consider the possibility of teaching yourself using instructional books or videos.

Following Through

Dedicate your time. There are many things you can do to help make the process easier and keep yourself focused. At the end of the day though, most goals are achieved by putting a lot of time and hard work into making them a reality. Think about how long you expect it to take to achieve your goal, and when you want it to be completed. For example, imagine you expect you'll need 40 hours of work to master the basics of playing guitar and you want learn it in a month. You'll need to spend a little over an hour on this every day.

There's no way to get around putting in the time. If you are truly committed to your goal, it is what you must do.

Make it a routine. One way to make putting in the time easier is to build your efforts into a daily routine. Schedule time to work on your goals into every day.

For example, you might spend a half an hour from 6:30 practicing musical scales. You could spend another half an hour from 6:30 to 7 practicing chords. You could spend 15 minutes from 7:15 learning to play a specific song. If you stuck to this every day (or even every other day), you could learn the basics of playing any instrument very quickly!

Track your progress. Once you start working toward your goal, keep track of your progress. Keep a journal, use an app, or get a desk calendar and make a note of time that you put in, sub-goals you've achieved, etc.

Tracking your progress can help you stay motivated by highlighting your successes. It can also help keep you accountable for sticking to your routine.

Keeping a journal in which you write about the process daily is also a good way to reduce stress you might feel about achieving your goals.

Stay motivated. One of the hardest parts of following through on a goal, especially in the long term, is staying motivated. Making achievable sub-goals and tracking your progress can both help. But, you may need to add some additional reinforcement.

Reinforcement means that you create consequences for your actions. There are two types of reinforcement.

Positive reinforcement means adding something to your life. For example, you might treat yourself to a celebratory dessert for achieving a sub-goal.

Negative reinforcement is when something is taken away. If that something is unwanted, that can be a reward. For example, you might allow yourself to skip a chore one week as a reward for reaching a sub-goal. This chore is "removed" from your life that week.

Reinforcement is more effective in keeping up your motivation than punishment. Depriving yourself of things or otherwise punishing yourself for failure is a bad idea. So, stick to rewards instead when possible.

Acknowledgments:

Some sections of this Book contained material adapted from.

As a Man Thinketh

By

James Allen

(public domain text)

Wikihow

(creative commons text)

Disclaimer:

This book is intended as helpful advice and support only, for educational purposes and is not intended to replace professional medical aid for diagnosed psychiatric conditions. The author advises anyone suffering debilitating depression to seek a professional medical/psychiatric diagnosis as soon as possible. The author hopes this work has been helpful.

Printed in Great Britain
by Amazon